Numerology, Amulets and Angels 2024

Alina A. Rubi and Angeline Rubi

Who does not own a lucky ring, a chain that never comes off, or an object that they would not give away for anything in the world? We all attribute a special power to certain items that belong to us and this distinctive character that they assume for us makes them magical objects.

For a talisman to act and influence circumstances, its wearer must have faith in it, and this will transform it into an immense object, able to fulfill everything that is asked of it.

In the everyday sense an amulet is any object that propitiates good as a preventive measure against evil, harm, disease, and witchcraft.

Amulets for good luck can help you to have a year 2024 full of blessings in your home, work, with your family, attract money and health. For the amulets to work properly you should not lend them to anyone else, and you should always have them at hand.

Amulets have existed in all cultures and are made from elements of nature that serve as catalysts of energies that help create human desires.

The amulet is assigned the power to ward off evils, spells, diseases, disasters or to counteract evil wishes cast through the eyes of others.

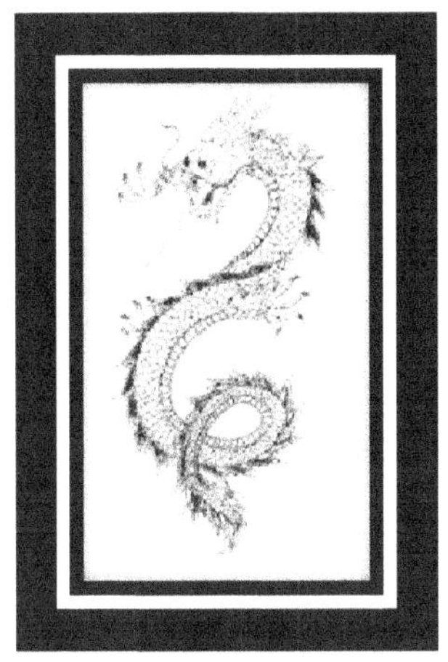

It is a carrier of energy, light, prosperity, fortune, and protection. In all Chinese traditions, myths, and fables there is a dragon as an emblem of steadfastness, tenacity, abundance, and magic.

Using it as an amulet or talisman will help you to have good luck. Having it in your home will make the spaces more harmonious and the energy will flow.

The dragon is a guardian of the divine, a protector of our home.

A home protected by a dragon, according to is a protected space, and full of good luck.

Taurus

Fleur de Lis.

It is a symbol used in Freemasonry, alchemy, and other religions. A symbol of naivety, dignity, and virginity.

It is an amulet that opens roads, a source of new opportunities for well-being.

The fleur-de-lis is a representation that does not exist in nature but is based on the image of a lily. It refers to the ideas of royalty and enlightenment.

It has a triangle base that alludes to water, and a cross that symbolizes spiritual realization, enlarged with two symmetrical leaves that wrap around a horizontal branch.

It represents wisdom, courage, and prosperity.

The fleur-de-lis, with its symbolism of purity and divinity, can serve as a reminder of our connection to the divine and the power of faith to transform and heal our lives.

It will help you face your emotions and inner conflicts, cleansing your heart of negative energies and promoting emotional balance.

Gemini

Archangel Michael.

The archangel Michael is the most famous of the archangels. He is the most invoked and the one most people ask for help. All this is because he is a spiritual warrior. You should use an image of St. Michael to invoke his blessings and to grant you strength and protection from evil forces.

This archangel will also help you find your life's purpose. Invoking him when you need help will give you the courage and determination you need. When you evoke him in times of distress, he helps you regain your calm.

When you call on him, he will intervene and fight for you so that you can get rid of the negativity.

The Ankh. Egyptian Cross.

The Egyptian cross, one of the oldest and most important amulets of Ancient Egypt, signifies life and immortality.

A talisman that will give you strength, abundance, and protection against bad luck. It is believed that the Egyptians used it as an amulet for good health. This was an amulet used during life and carried to the grave.

It has magical properties and is also known as "the Egyptian key of wisdom". It has the power to help people understand all the secrets of the universe.

This protective amulet is a repellent of evil and negative energies.

Leo

Unicorn.

The unicorn symbolizes the hope for healing and the strength we all seek. The Unicorn can be used to amplify your psychic gifts.

The unicorn represents purity, unconditional love, and magic. This mythological creature has been revered for its divine strength and for being a source of energy that allows us to connect with the spiritual realm. The presence of the unicorn in your life will remind you that magic and love are always present, and that you are strong. It is an animal that attracts good luck and justice. As a symbol of purity and will protect and guard you from all evil.

Celtic Cross.

The Celtic Cross symbolizes the desire to discover and experience the mysteries of life and is a compass that will guide you through your spiritual journey.

It reflects the hope that the Celts had, and one of the Celtic pieces with more symbolism and power in magic. It represents knowledge, strength, compassion, and infinite love.

The mystical, the divine and the sacred harmonize in this symbol, used in many civilizations as an amulet. It is a powerful good luck charm. It is protective, and if you wear it you will have peace, harmony, balance, and wisdom.

Eye of Horus

It is a talisman that protects the wearer from disease, from the dangers that lie in wait, and from the evil eye.

The Eye of Horus symbolizes health, prosperity, and the ability to be reborn. It is a protective shield against bad luck and toxic energies that reach us.

In addition, it allows prosperity and happiness to enter and override any darkness or curse.

In addition to its benefits as a protector, it contains all the mathematical symbols with which the Ancient Egyptians represented fractions.

It is an incredibly positive amulet that you can use to protect yourself from evil and attract positive energies to your personal space. It purifies the body from toxicity and bad energies and will help you find inner peace.

It balances and repairs what is broken or weakened, that is, it increases well-being. It is a symbol of renewal that is used to improve physical and mental health.

It represents the power of the eternal, which does not change with time. It will help you to achieve position and stability, giving firmness to your goals. It provides strength, courage, and wisdom.

Clover

It is one of the most powerful amulets, for centuries magical powers have been attributed to this type of plant, its popularity dates to Celtic culture, but it is a popular symbol of good luck in many cultures. The Egyptians carried amulets in the shape of a four-leaf clover to protect themselves from misfortunes, dangers, disasters, and mishaps.

According to legends, each leaf has a meaning. The first is fame, the second wealth, the third love and the fourth health.

It is related to fortune because it is used to get money.

As it is a protective amulet, it will keep away evil spirits and eyes from your life.

As the plant is difficult to obtain, you can have its design captured in diverse ways. One of the easiest is in jewelry.

Horse

Horses are considered symbols of wealth. In ancient times horses were given as gifts to emperors and kings because they are symbols of triumph and success.

Horses signify power, strength, and courage. They are a symbol of speed, courage, and perseverance.

They are associated with the Fire element and represent fame, freedom and achievement of goals that require your energetic strength.

You can put ornaments with the figure of a horse, or several in the living room, study, office or if you work at home place it on your desk. As it is considered an amulet to attract success and good luck it must be near you.

Capricorn

Sword

This amulet keeps away bad energies and gives you protection against your enemies. It is used against envy and the evil eye, as it has a great power to protect us from any evil that envious people wish us.

It absorbs bad energies, so if you wear it, your health will be safe. In addition to warding off negativity, it is believed to bring well-being and love.

It will also protect you against black magic.

Caravaca Cross

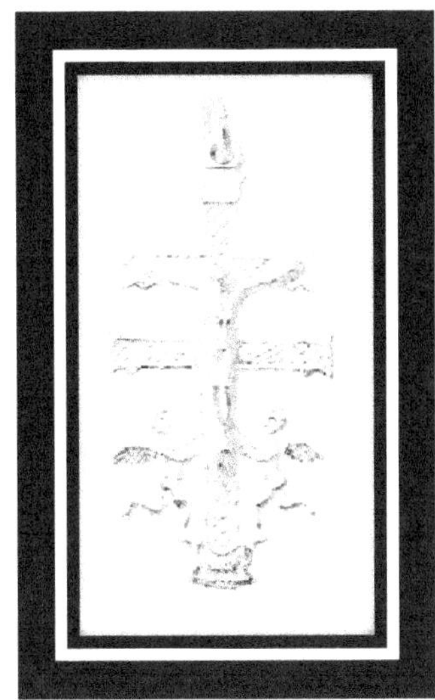

This is one of the oldest amulets and the one that offers the most protection. Its symbolism is very deep, and it resides in its history, appearance, and shape.

This cross project a powerful protective power, for that reason it serves as protection against the bad energies that exist around you.

Its power became the key element in exorcism rituals, since only its presence can expel any dark entity.

This amulet will protect your economy giving you prosperity, you can use it to get your partner back, improve at work and help you balance your life by attracting good luck.

Horseshoe.

One of the oldest amulets in history, it is a magical symbol and a talisman.

Since ancient Greece, horseshoes have been considered powerful amulets that protected from evil and attracted good luck. Their shape, evoking the crescent moon, symbolizes fertility and prosperity.

If you want it to bring you good luck, turn it upside down, but if, on the contrary, you are looking for protection, turn it upside down. Its power is to help dispel doubts and attract good fortune.

Lucky Quartz for each Zodiac Sign in 2024

We are all attracted to diamonds, rubies, emeralds and sapphires, obviously precious stones. Semi-precious stones such as carnelian, tiger's eye, white quartz, and lapis lazuli are also highly prized as they have been used as ornaments and symbols of power for thousands of years.

What many do not know is that they were valued for more than their beauty: each had a sacred significance, and their healing properties were as important as their ornamental value.

Crystals still have the same properties in our days, most people are familiar with the most popular ones such as amethyst, malachite and obsidian, but nowadays there are new crystals such as larimar, petalite and phenacite that have become known.

A crystal is a solid body with a geometrically regular shape, crystals were formed when the earth was created and have continued to metamorphose as the planet has changed, crystals are the DNA of the earth, they are miniature stores that contain the development of our planet over millions of years.

Some have been bent to extraordinary pressures and others grew in chambers buried deep underground, others dripped into being. Whatever form they take, their crystalline structure can absorb, conserve, focus and emit energy.

At the heart of the crystal is the atom, its electrons, and protons. The atom is dynamic and is composed of a series of particles that rotate around the center in constant motion, so that, although the crystal may seem motionless, it is a living molecular mass that vibrates at a certain frequency, and this is what gives energy to the crystal.

Gems used to be a royal and priestly prerogative, the priests of Judaism wore a plaque on their chest full of precious stones which was much more than an emblem to designate their function, as it transferred power to the wearer.

Men have worn stones since the stone age as they had a protective function guarding their wearers from various evils. Today's crystals have the same power, and we can select our jewelry not only according to their external attractiveness, having them near us can boost our energy (orange carnelian), clean the space around us (amber) or attract wealth (citrine).

Certain crystals such as smoky quartz and black tourmaline could absorb negativity, emitting a pure and clean energy.

Wearing a black tourmaline around the neck protects from electromagnetic emanations including that of cell phones, a citrine will not only attract wealth, but will also help you keep it, place it in the wealthy part of your home (the back left most away from the front door).

If you are looking for love, crystals can help you, place a rose quartz in the relationship corner of your house (the back right corner furthest away from the front door) its effect is so powerful that you may want to add an amethyst to offset the attraction.

You can also use rhodochrosite, love will come your way.

Crystals can heal and give balance, some crystals contain minerals known for their therapeutic properties, malachite has a high concentration of copper, wearing a malachite bracelet allows the body to absorb minimal amounts of copper.

Lapis lazuli relieves migraine, but if the headache is caused by stress, amethyst, amber or turquoise placed above the eyebrows will relieve it.

Quartz and minerals are jewels of mother earth, give yourself the opportunity, and connect with the magic they give off.

Lucky Quartz for Aries

Ruby *is the stone associated with this sign. Aries who wear this stone can receive the benefits of having good blood circulation.*

With the ruby you will receive success and wealth, as well as courage, encouragement, and loyalty. In the Republic of the Union of Myanmar, where this stone comes from, it is considered to attract friends and happiness.

For the Japanese and Chinese, it brings health and longevity, regulates the passions, drives away evil thoughts, and guarantees peace and health. Other stones related to Aries are red jasper and fire agate.

Lucky Quartz for Taurus

Smoky Quartz*. It is a divine symbol on this physical plane. This mystical quartz will give you a lot of light. It is the quartz of mediums, spiritualists, and alchemists because it breaks all the negative. It is associated with the psychic plane, it is the most primitive in the world, and it is an oracle.*

It will protect you against the most adverse energies such as envy, anger, and destructive thoughts.

It is the most effective energy healer on the planet, evaporates, enhances, protects, and molds energy, and is miraculous in unblocking it. It transforms the energy to the purest state admitted.

Lucky Quartz for Gemini

White quartz or rock crystal.

An energy receiver par excellence, and amplifier of positive vibrations at all levels. It helps with mental concentration and reinforces or enhances the other quartz. It is the most used therapeutically.

It symbolizes happiness and is sometimes used to honor a birth or to offer peace after death. Its main function is to bring balance and peace by mobilizing or deactivating energies.

It will help you resist bad moments, negative thoughts such as guilt, or emotional problems. It also protects you from fears and anxieties. Its healing properties improve cognition and enhance mental agility. It helps to make memory faster and to learn as it increases knowledge and the faculty of listening.

With this crystal, you will become patient.

Lucky Quartz for Cancer

Onyx

A protective quartz that cleanses the aura. According to legend, this stone emerged when Venus was sleeping and Cupid cut her nails, so that they fell to the ground and these nails were transmuted into wonderful stones that were baptized Onyx.

In times of stress, it helps to make prudent decisions, and to achieve your professional goals if you use it as an amulet.

It is a powerful stone, with psychological benefits that make it an admirable choice to provide support for people suffering from anxiety. Its properties will connect you with your spiritual guides, and you will be able to see everything more clearly.

Lucky Quartz for Leo

Carnelian

Positive quartz for those who have trouble concentrating, who are mentally alienated or complicated in life. It gives courage and protection. It is indicated for melancholic people.

It is used as a talisman in homes and businesses as a defense against the evil eye, and envy. It is connected to the energy of authority and passion.

It is recommended for professional success, to reassure doubts and to give mental clarity when a professional decision must be made.

For those who find it difficult to speak in public, carnelian helps them to have the courage to face this obstacle. It is suggested for those who have nervous problems, since the energetic projection of the quartz helps to achieve sleep and be calm, therefore, it favors physical and mental rest.

Lucky Quartz for Virgo

Jade

It functions as a protective energy in the place where it is found. It is associated with stability and security. This quartz is beneficial to have it in a specific place because when we carry it with us it can cause discord with our friends or colleagues.

It helps you to think positive, symbolizes peace, and introspection. This quartz will give you all the strength you need to move forward. It is a stone that will help you to release all the emotions that block you, and to see life with positive lenses. It helps with the proper functioning of the kidneys, heart, and stomach.

There are several colors of jade: blue and green jade, signifying peace, and reflection. Brown jade, related to the earth element, and productivity. Green jade, accelerates the nervous system, moving us to a state of peace in which we can eliminate any negative feelings we feel. Orange jade helps in emotional management, red jade, used to channel tensions and solve problems in harmony. White Jade is the perfect help to make decisions and to know which direction is the perfect one. Yellow Jade brings us joy and helps us to relate to others.

Lucky Quartz for Libra

Rose quartz

It raises self-esteem. It is used in children who need love to stabilize their energy centers. It is used to attract love and works as an instrument to balance your emotional side with your heart rate.

It is the necessary complement in your spiritual journey, a quartz with an extraordinary power that can bring you improvements in your health. This quartz is famous for its strength, and for being one of the most effective stones when it comes to healing.

It can absorb negative energies and replace them with positive ones, thanks to its vibrations. These energies are responsible for opening your Heart Chakra.

Lucky Quartz for Scorpio

Citrine

A super magnetic quartz. It will give you a strong personal charisma and help you to be creative.

Its vibrations will give you energy, abundance, and economic prosperity.

If you want to expand the prosperity in your life you should place citrine somewhere in your home, or business, where you relate to the economic world. Its energies will increase the possibilities of your success.

It works as a defensive talisman, capable of neutralizing any kind of negative energy.

It provides intuition so that you can protect yourself properly.

Project joy and harmonious feelings to all those around you.

It will help you to gradually improve your self-esteem and find your identity. It will transform your value system so that you can feel motivated.

Agate

A quartz with great energetic power. It helps to increase self-esteem and transforms negative energies into positive ones.

It helps emotional, mental, and physical stability. It is good for migraines, relieves all kinds of physical ailments, such as muscle, joint and bone pain.

It is known as the stone of confidence. It will bring you wealth and abundance in all areas of your life.

It helps to develop creativity, and security. It is also assigned powers to evade curses.

If you place it under your pillow, you will not have problems to sleep, you will avoid insomnia, stress at night, or anxieties.

It will give you a calculating mentality.

It acts as an amulet so that things go well, and you obtain prosperity in a brief period.

To take advantage of the protective qualities of this quartz you should always have it with you.

Lucky Quartz for Capricorn

Fluorite

It helps with mental instabilities, giving harmony to the person who uses it.

It helps in reconciliations and allows to see clearly the truths hidden behind the masks.

It also facilitates intellectual and emotional well-being. It is used for the treatment of colds, herpes, and ulcers.

It is a stone with protective powers, at the spiritual level. It purifies the aura and stops manipulation.

It is noted for fostering intuitive faculties, makes you more knowledgeable of higher spiritual existences, and stimulates spiritual awakening.

Lucky Quartz for Aquarius

Obsidian

A powerful protective quartz. It consolidates energies and exposes to light all the dark aspects of a person. Increases attraction to a different sex and promotes peace.

It is a magical and divine quartz. It is known by the name of black velvet, it is great against uncertainty and mental blockages, as it absorbs negative energies.

It will give you the power to perceive your doubts and dark thoughts, the issues that you have rejected you will be pressured to solve them, and you will do it in a calm way.

With this stone you can face any circumstance with courage, it will keep away all kinds of negativity, and will function as a mirror in which your own insecurities will be reflected.

Lucky Quartz for Pisces

Amethyst

It is a protective stone that works at the level of intuition, developing the third eye and stimulating wisdom.

It has the power to calm anger and destroy its negative emotions.

It cancels mental chaos and brings peace, for that reason it is used to generate emotional balance.

It is used to reduce stress and anxiety.

It can also help people in distress with the strong emotions that come out during that cycle.

This quartz calms emotional storms, and in scenarios of danger, amethyst will come to your assistance.

It offers courage to the wearer and is an efficient amulet.

If you use it, you will be protected against sufferings and dangers.

The Angels are beings of light, their mission is to help us to evolve and to protect us from dangers.

All people are protected by an Angel, or several Angels, according to their date of birth. Your guardian Angel assures you success in love, work, and other areas of your life.

Sometimes we are so deep in a life with so much stress, that we forget that we are accompanied by beings of light, who are waiting for us to ask for help.

When we are aware of their presence and decide to enjoy the gift of having them in our lives, our world is filled with magic.

This 2024 Angel Horoscope has many spiritual messages for you. If you feel lost, or if you are wondering what your mission is this year 2024, here you can find the answers.

If you bought this book, it is because the universe is trying to tell you what to do and where to go. All you need is to discover the hidden messages that the Angels have sent you inside this book.

Angels have existed for thousands of years, in diverse cultures and civilizations. They have special powers and have contributed to human evolution, changes, and development of our society. The Guardian Angels will be present in your life during 2024 to protect you, strengthen your connections with the spiritual world, and to give you many miracles.

Archangel for your Zodiac Sign

Each zodiac sign has an Archangel mentor who oversees it.

When the time comes to reincarnate, we select the most appropriate zodiac sign to learn the life lessons that will bring us more experiences for our evolution.

The Archangels help us to choose the sign of the zodiac to fulfill the purposes of our soul.

Aries. Archangel Chamuel

The Archangel Chamuel means "the one who sees God", he is related to initiatives and passion, two super strong qualities in people of the Aries sign. This sign is tireless and does not stop until it achieves its goals.

The Archangel Chamuel gives Aries the power of decision and enthusiasm to accomplish his goals. This Archangel is also known as Samael, Chamuel or Camuel, and is the Angel of harmony, confidence, power, and diversity.

This Archangel gives the Aries sign an assertive and reliable personality.

Aries is an extroverted sign, impetuous and enthusiastic when it comes to taking on challenges. They are impatient and easily annoyed, but they are not resentful.

To Archangel Chamuel belongs the Golden Ray, the planet Mars, and the day Tuesday.

Archangel Chamuel's message for Aries is:

Only the energy of love within a purpose gives lasting value and benefit.

Rose quartz is related to the healing energies of Archangel Chamuel, and you can use them to heal yourself emotionally by invoking his name, or his presence, because he specializes in emotional healing.

Archangel Chamuel oversees all the Angels of Love. They give Aries when he asks for it, compassion, and love. Chamuel can help you with your relationships, specifically if you have conflicts, emotional complications, or breakups. Archangel Chamuel can help you find your soul or twin flame and in all circumstances that demand spontaneous communication.

Chamuel can help you build solid and healthy structures, improve your abilities to love, so that you have the capacity to give and receive love completely without conditions.

Chamuel dissolves feelings of low self-esteem, helps you find your purpose and soul mission.

The Archangel Chamuel represents the strength to face and overcome challenges in our lives. If you do not know what you want, Chamuel will move you to environments that will bring you peace, helping you to release tensions and stress. Archangel Chamuel is the protector of the weak and the humiliated.

As the Archangel Chamuel sees in all directions of time, i.e., three-dimensionally, he can help you find things you have lost.

Invoke the Archangel Chamuel if you feel sad, he will help you heal, relieve your pain and your inability to forgive.

To invoke or evoke help to heal emotionally with Archangel Chamuel you must light pink candles or put pink roses to ask for healing.

All Archangels have an exclusive place in the etheric plane of the Earth, and you can find their sanctuaries through meditation or in your dreams. The etheric temple of Archangel Chamuel is in St. Louis, Missouri, United States.

Taurus. Archangel Haniel

The Archangel Haniel rules the sign of Taurus, he refers to the characteristics of wholeness, confidence, and pragmatism. The Archangel Haniel's name means 'grace of God' and he is the Angel of intellectuality.

Haniel is related to the planet Venus, and the day Friday.

Taurus is a sign that loves material comfort, enjoys luxury, and quality goods. They are prosperous in many areas, but especially in finances.

Taurus is a very controlling sign that must learn patience. They possess a natural inclination towards stability but must be careful not to fall into the trap of materialism.

The Archangel Haniel is also known as Anael, Anafiel, and Daniel. His colors are orange and white.

This Archangel is related to the white and orange Ray.

Haniel has an energy that motivates us to seek spiritual wisdom, being also the Angel of Celestial Communication works with group energies and speakers. He is an Archangel related to the Moon that is why he connects with us through visualizations and recurring dreams. Archangel Haniel helps transmute dark vibrations and energies and offers protection. He is with us in new beginnings when transitional stages happen in our lives.

This Archangel brings inspiration to our lives, teaches lessons and oversees spiritual healing, and diverse types of religions. Archangel Haniel retrieves lost secrets, harmonizes relationships, and brings beauty in everything. Haniel heals envy, anger, and jealousy.

Archangel Haniel provides you with information about your profession, and relationships. He assists you in your spiritual journey and urges you to seek your life's purpose. He urges you to look within yourself and find your personal truth because in this way you can stand up for yourself.

Archangel Haniel helps you to live in the present, see reality and recognize your talents and abilities.

Archangel Haniel reminds you that it is your responsibility to be healthy mentally and physically. This Archangel is related to healing through quartz and essential oils, which is why he oversees homeopathic physicians. This powerful Archangel possesses the power to transform sadness into happiness.

This Archangel works with imbalances in the energy field and brings healing on an emotional, spiritual, and physical level.

This is a warrior Archangel who helps us fulfill our soul's purpose, guiding us through revelations, visions, and angelic synchronicities.

When you feel confused or depressed, invoke the Archangel Haniel to give you the gift of perseverance.

Gemini. Archangel Raphael

Gemini is protected by the Archangel Raphael, which is why this zodiac sign is so adaptable and sociable.

Raphael is one of the main healing angels and guides the healers.

Archangel Raphael rules the planet Mercury and the day Wednesday.

People of the Gemini sign are highly intelligent, their most valuable tool is their mind. Gemini is very versatile, and this attitude drains his energies leading him sometimes to nervous exhaustion and anxiety. Gemini people have an insatiable thirst for learning and their minds are very curious.

Archangel Raphael is related to the Green Ray. Raphael's healing powers are focused on dissolving blockages by transmuting them into love.

Archangel Raphael is known to be the chief of the Guardian Angels and is the patron of medicine, hence he is also called the Archangel of Knowledge.

Raphael is also the patron saint of travelers and assists in the spiritual and physical healing not only of humans, but also of animals.

This Archangel Raphael can help you develop your intuition and enhance your creative visualization. It puts you in touch with your personal spirituality and allows you to find healing in nature. Emerald is the healing quartz related to Archangel Raphael.

Archangel Raphael works in your subconscious so that you can free yourself from fear and darkness. The Healing Angels team is led by Archangel Raphael, these energies of Archangel Raphael and his Healing Angels can be invoked in hospitals and in circumstances where there is a sick person who is not known to have an illness.

Archangel Raphael focuses his healing energies on dissolving blockages in the chakras that cause disease and helps to eliminate addictions.

Rafael heals the wounds of past lives, erasing all inherited family karmas.

You can call Archangel Raphael every time you, another person has a physical illness, he will intervene directly and guide you to effect healing.

Archangel Raphael reminds you that it is through forgiveness that healing occurs, and he is intricately connected to the healers of light. Raphael ensures that all that is necessary appears to facilitate successful healing.

Call upon Archangel Raphael to protect and guide you, he will help you to cleanse your energies and focus. To invoke the healing power of Archangel Raphael, light green or yellow candles and you will receive instant results.

Archangel Raphael is not restricted by the limitations of time and space, being able to be simultaneously with all who invoke his presence. He comes to your side the instant you ask for help.

Cancer - Archangel Gabriel

The Archangel Gabriel protects the sign of Cancer. He rules on Monday.

Cancer is supervised is a very empathetic and sensitive sign. They look gentle, but they are active. Family is the most important thing for Cancer.

The Archangel Gabriel is known as the Angel of the Resurrection, the Angel of harmony and joy. He announced the birth of Jesus Christ and communicated with Joan of Arc.

Archangel Gabriel teaches you to seek angelic help through meditation and dreams and takes care of humanity.

Gabriel is the Archangel of the mind, you can call on him when you have mental challenges, to help you make decisions.

Archangel Gabriel is the protector of emotions, and creativity. When we struggle with abuse, addictions, dysfunctional families, and to have love it is Archangel Gabriel that we must invoke.

Archangel Gabriel offers you spirituality and uplifts your spirit. He alerts you to be aware of the energies around you.

Gabriel knows your soul purpose and mission; his mission is to help you understand what your contract obligations are in this incarnation.

Archangel Gabriel increases creativity, optimism, transmutes fears and gives you motivation. Gabriel cleanses and raises your vibrations, guides you in your life and helps you to live faithfully, honoring your talents and abilities.

Gabriel reminds you that everyone contributes to the development of humanity by being who they are. He wants you to be firm in your convictions.

This Archangel will help you to know the truth in conflict situations, he will give you more intuition and insight.

Archangel Gabriel is an Angel of knowledge, has connection with spiritual leaders, and instructs us on what our talents are and shows you the symbols of your soul's mission so that you will be able to attract perfect connections and opportunities.

Call upon Archangel Gabriel to cleanse and purify your body and mind of negative thoughts. Call upon him for help with all forms of communication, including the ability to speak and make new friends.

Leo - Archangel Michael

Michael the Archangel is the chief of the heavenly armies and protects the sign of Leo. His name means the one who is like God, and he is the symbol of justice. He is considered the greatest of all the Archangels.

Archangel Michael collaborates with the Blue Ray and rules the day on Sunday. Michael helps with communication and is known as the Prince of Archangels.

Leo is a sign that has excellent organizational skills, and they are always willing to fight to succeed. They are competitive and loyal to their loved ones.

Archangel Michael helps you to be aware of your thoughts and feelings and encourages you to act. Michael offers you protection, self-confidence, strength, and unconditional love.

Archangel Michael is charged with freeing us from fear, negativity, dramas, and intimidation. This Archangel is charged with dismantling all dysfunctional structures, such as corrupt government systems and financial organizations.

Michael is the protector of all humanity; you can call on him to strengthen you to change direction and find your purpose. Call Michael if you feel a lack of motivation.

This Archangel works for cooperation and harmony with others, and specializes in removing energetic implants, and cutting the ties that paralyze us.

Michael helps us to stand up for our truths without compromising our principles, he brings peace and when we are ready to discard old concepts and beliefs, Archangel Michael supports us by cutting the ties that bind us negatively and prevent us from developing our potential.

Archangel Michael guides those who feel stuck in their profession and helps us to discover the light within us by giving us courage when we face tricky situations.

Ask Archangel Michael to cut the energetic cords that bind you to situations, toxic people, behavioral patterns, and harmful emotions.

People who connect with Archangel Michael are powerful, strong, and empathetic. Invoke Archangel Michael to protect your home and family, he always comes when we need strength to overcome a challenging conflict.

You can visit their temples during meditation, or sleep, in the etheric realm above the Canadian Rockies.

Virgo - Archangel Raphael

Archangel Raphael protects the sign of Virgo and rules the day on Wednesday. He is one of the main Angels of healing and offers his attributes of efficiency and analytical mentality to the sixth sign of the zodiac.

Virgo is always attentive to details because they like to examine all options before deciding. Sometimes they are shy and do not like to draw attention to themselves.

Archangel Raphael rules Ray #4, the green ray, and is known as the head of the Guardian Angels. He helps develop intuition and helps us open our hearts to the healing powers of the Universe.

Raphael puts you in touch with your spirituality and allows you to find healing in the universal energies. He is known as the physician of the angelic realm as he can direct his healing powers towards the dissolution of negative blockages, and illnesses.

Raphael can be called upon to heal we, and to heal others. Raphael helps to heal relationships and remove addictions. He supports light workers and

and guides us to make positive changes in life.

To invoke him, light green candles. You can visit his temples during meditation or sleep on the etheric plane above Fatima, Portugal.

Libra - Archangel Haniel

Libra is a sign protected by the Archangel Haniel, rules the planet Venus, and the day Friday.

Libra is an impartial sign that always seeks balance between soul, mind, and spirit. They are diplomatic, stable, and balanced. Diplomacy is their most outstanding characteristic as they can see both sides of a conflict, but they are a bit paralyzed when making decisions.

The meaning of the Archangel Haniel is the glory of God, and he connects with us through dreams. He offers us protection, and harmony. Haniel assists us in positive changes, new beginnings, and fosters balance in transitions.

Haniel rules peace, brings inspiration and helps to heal envy and jealousy.

Archangel Haniel motivates us to live in the present moment and to see the reality within ourselves. He encourages us to take care of ourselves and reminds us that we are responsible for being mentally and spiritually healthy. He has the power to transform sadness into happiness and encourages us to respect our own natural rhythms.

Invoke Archangel Haniel to find balance, make your intentions come true and release negative energies. He will help you stay calm during notable events by strengthening your confidence. Haniel empowers spiritual gifts and psychic abilities and reminds us that we are divine beings. He is a warrior Angel, turn to him when you need spiritual support or when you feel emotionally weak, he will give you determination, and the energy to trust your intuition.

Scorpion - Archangel Chamuel and Azrael

Scorpio is protected by the Archangels Azrael and Chamuel. Azrael is an Angel who rules the planet Pluto and Chamuel rules the planet Mars and Tuesday.

Those under the influence of Scorpio are given powerful and intense personalities.

Scorpio has a paranoid personality and is obsessed with what is going on in their lives. They cling tightly to what is theirs and refuse to give in without a fight.

The Archangel Azrael's name means whom God helps, he rules Ray #2 which contains vibrations of love and wisdom. Azrael is often referred to as the Angel of Death and that name reminds us that death is transformation.

Archangel Azrael's purpose is to help those who are in transition from physical life to spiritual life. He possesses much compassion and wisdom and has universal healing energies, for those who are grieving the loss of a loved one.

Archangel Azrael comforts people before their physical death and ensures that they do not suffer during their death, surrounding bereaved family and friends with healing energies.

Invoke Archangel Azrael to comfort a loved one and convey messages of love to the spiritual realm. Azrael can help you go through the stages of grief with acceptance.

Azrael helps to create space in our lives for new energies to come in.

Sagittarius - Archangel Zadkiel

Sagittarius is protected by the Archangel Zadkiel, who works with the Violet Ray, rules the planet Jupiter, and on Thursday.

Sagittarius is optimistic and intuitive by nature, but sometimes they cross the boundaries of reality.

Zadkiel's name means the righteousness of God, but it is also related to darkness, inertia. It helps us to discover the divine aspects within us and to develop skills that serve our life's purposes.

Zadkiel is the Archangel of freedom and forgiveness, he assists in spiritual awakening, bestows blessings, and gifts you with discernment. Use the Violet Flame to invoke the Archangel Zadkiel, it will help you to meditate, and develop your intuition. Zadkiel can be invoked to bring forgiveness to others. He leads the Angels of Mercy and can help you to be tolerant and diplomatic.

The healing energies of Archangel Zadkiel and his Angels of Joy will always help you transform memories, break through limitations, erase energetic blockages, and get rid of addictions. Zadkiel encourages you to love and forgive without fear and reminds you to love yourself, and others, unconditionally.

The Archangel Zadkiel is the energetic source behind poverty and wealth and all their manifestations, so he is associated with luck and chance. Zadkiel reminds you that good and bad luck are earned by each individual person, and he values fortune accordingly.

Archangel Zadkiel is responsible for the beginnings and endings of things; he can be called upon to bring an end to a painful situation. Archangel Zadkiel helps us find the inner courage to do the right thing for ourselves, and for others.

To connect with Archangel Zadkiel, use violet-colored candles, or amethyst quartz. Archangel Zadkiel is associated with the Ascended Master Saint Germain, and protects mystics,

Archangel Zadkiel and Saint Amethyst have their etheric retreat, called the Temple of Purification on the island of Cuba.

Zadkiel heals emotional wounds and painful memories, increases your self-esteem, and helps you develop your natural talents and skills.

If you want more tolerance in conflicting situations, turn to Archangel Zadkiel, he will transmute everything dark and raise your vibration.

Capricorn - Archangel Uriel

Capricorn is protected by the Archangel Uriel. This Archangel means Fire of God, rules the Red Ray, and is associated with light, lightning, and thunder.

Uriel can show us how we can heal our lives, help us to understand the concept of karma, and to understand why things are the way they are. Uriel relates to divine magic, problem solving, spiritual understanding, and helps us realize our potential.

Uriel should be invoked when you are working with issues related to economics and politics. You can also invoke him for greater intuition.

Uriel helps you release your fears and opens the channels for divine communication, promotes peace, helps release our obsessive behavior patterns and brings practical solutions.

Uriel can be called upon for intellectual work, and to recognize the light within us.

Archangel Uriel has his etheric retreat in the Tatra Mountains in Poland, and you can ask to be taken there to have your fears healed.

Aquarius - Archangel Uriel

Aquarius is protected by the Archangel Uriel, giving this sign a humanitarian character.

Uriel works with the Ruby Ray and rules the planet Uranus.

Aquarius is independent, and progressive. Archangel Uriel helps with problem solving and finding solutions and is one of the most powerful Archangels.

Uriel helps to release energy blockages in the body, and since he is known as the Angel of Salvation, he can show us how we can heal our lives, finding blessings in adversity, turning defeats into victories, and releasing painful burdens.

Uriel is the Angel of transformation, creativity, and divine order, he rules the missionaries, and is the guardian of the writers. He is the interpreter of prophecies, and of our dreams. He impels us to take responsibility for our lives and brings transforming energies to our minds.

Archangel Uriel is invoked for clarity and intuition. He works to develop in us the qualities of mercy and compassion.

He offers protection, teaches selfless service, and promotes cooperation.

The Archangel Uriel clears old fears and replaces them with wisdom, propitiates vital enlightenment for those who feel they have lost their way and who have emotions related to abandonment and suicide.

Archangel Uriel works to eradicate fear and restore hope, and always seeks to protect the welfare of people who are unable to exercise their free will.

Call upon Archangel Uriel to help you develop your full potential and protect you from envy.

You can ask to visit his temples during your meditation sessions or in your dreams.

Archangel Uriel has his etheric retreat in the Tatra Mountains in Poland.

Pisces - Archangel Azrael and Zadkiel

The sign of Pisces is protected and supervised by the Archangel Azrael and the Archangel Zadkiel.

Archangel Azrael rules the planet Neptune and Archangel Zadkiel rules the planet Jupiter and Thursday. Zadkiel works in the Violet Ray.

Pisces tend to be idealistic, and sensitive; they love to be in love. Every aspect of life should have some romance in it.

Archangel Zadkiel is the guardian of the Violet Flame, which has a super high vibratory frequency.

Archangel Zadkiel is known as the Angel of Understanding and Compassion and is related to darkness, contemplation, and nurturing.

Zadkiel is on a mission to help you with spiritual awakening, he bestows blessings that are designed through faith to increase understanding.

Using the Violet Flame, Archangel Zadkiel helps you to meditate, and increases your psychic abilities. Zadkiel helps open our minds and gives us psychic protection.

Zadkiel encourages tolerance and helps people to love themselves and connects us to our soul's mission.

Archangel Zadkiel brings healing to our emotional wounds, frees us, and motivates people to show mercy to others.

Working with Zadkiel increases your self-esteem and helps you remember and develop your natural talents, skills, and abilities. Call Zadkiel if you need help remembering specific details and facts.

Call upon Archangel Zadkiel to help you heal and transcend your negative emotions and improve your mental functions.

The Archangel Zadkiel is the energy behind poverty and wealth, and all their manifestations, so he is related to chance. Zadkiel imparts justice without prejudice, but is merciful to those who deserve it, he is responsible for beginnings and endings, and you can call on him whenever you want to end a chaotic circumstance.

Archangel Zadkiel can break through blocked or stagnant energies caused by anger and guilt.

Zadkiel and the Holy Amethyst have their etheric sanctuary on the island of Cuba.

Angel protector of your Zodiac Sign

Many times, we feel alone, without physical and emotional protection. Even if you cannot see it, your guardian Angel or spiritual guides are always with you, since the day you were born, protecting you. Invoke the name of your Angel in the moments when you feel you need help or advice, choose to put your life in their hands and they will lead you on the best path.

Aries. Angel Anauel

This Angel confers to the sign Aries an indestructible health and protection against the dark forces of evil, among them envy. Aries has an inflexible personality, they get desperate and angry very quickly, but their compassion and susceptibility opens all doors for them. This Guardian Angel is also known as Haniel, or Ariel. It is the Angel of creativity and sensuality. He arranges the success in couples, love and prevents the sufferings of the heart.

Taurus. Angel Uriel

Uriel will always come into your life when you need him for exams, medical studies, and when you have separation problems. Uriel will always protect your spirit and enlighten your mind so you can make the right decisions.

Gemini. Angel Eyael

Eyael will always protect you from adversities and free you from injustices, especially in the place where you work. This Angel is incredibly special of him, he knows with whom it is good for you to relate, that is, he will make you surround yourself with influential people who will help you succeed. This Angel encourages you to always look at the positive side of things and encourages your feelings of generosity and desire to help others.

Cancer. Angel Rochel

Rochel endows the Cancer sign with excellent vision to detect dangers, as well as creativity and talents to discover hidden secrets. He will destroy all your fears and your enemies. ask him to give you clarity, shrewdness and cunning.

Leo. Angel Nelkhael

Nelkhael will keep sadness and low self-esteem away from you. He will guard you from people who slander you out of envy and will help you to keep your commitments and assume your responsibilities. The problems of your daily life will be easier to cope with under his influence. Nelkhael offers you support in your darkest and saddest moments.

Virgo. Angel Melahel

Melahel when invoked will drive away violence from your life and your environment. This Angel will provide an energy that will drive back your enemies or make you invisible. He is also related to harmony and healing. He will bring you ways to connect with the universe and enjoy the secrets of nature.

Libra. Angel Yerathel

Yerathel offers the sign of Libra a lot of intelligence and insight to be able to detect your enemies. This Angel provides you with lucidity and reflective capacity, characteristics that will allow you to surround yourself with the right people. Yerathel gives you the weapons of justice and allows you to be wise and tolerant. By invoking Yerathel, you will achieve success.

Scorpion. Angel Azrael

Azrael*, known as the Archangel of death, will rescue you from injustice and at the same time renew your image and hopes. He reminds you that the universe loves you, he will guide you on the path of love, tenderness, and harmony at home. If you want to meet the right partner to create a lasting relationship and start a family, invoke this, Angel.*

Sagittarius. Umabel Angel

Umabel *repels envy from your relationships, and feelings that can harm you such as anger, jealousy, and hatred. He gives you the eloquence necessary for a calm and distinct expression. He gives you the art of persuasion. You know how to tip the scales in your favor, improve your communication skills so you know how to explain important things. He helps you make the right decisions, at the right time.*

Capricorn. Angel Sitael

Sitael, build shields around you, organize your life, and if you do not know which path to take, think about it and you will instantly focus. If you wish to improve your economic situation, cure yourself of an illness, or move, change, invoke this Angel and wait for the miracle.

Aquarius. Angel Gabriel

Gabriel will fight day by day, so that you can fight your battles. If you want help because there are people who want to harm you or put you in danger, ask this Angel for protection. If you are afraid that someone will commit an injustice against you, by invoking this Angel you will surely neutralize your enemy.

Pisces. Angel Daniel

Daniel will always keep you safe from illness and physical pain, you will always come out of all the mishaps and accidents that come your way.

Angelic Numbers and their Meanings

We are evolving spiritually, and every day the numerical sequences are seen by more people. These messages that come from a higher source, that is, from our Angels or spiritual guides, have the purpose of guiding you.

The Angels want to get our attention and communicate with us through these numbers in sequence. This is how they help us heal our lives. Unfortunately, some ignore these signs thinking they are coincidences when it is synchronicity.

Your Angels send you messages through number sequences, they may very subtly whisper in your ear so that you look at a specific place and notice the time on the clock, or the number on an advertisement. They show you meaningful number sequences in a physical way, by placing a car in front of you when you are standing in traffic that has a specific license plate number.

When you notice a numerical sequence repeating itself, ask the Angels what they are trying to tell you, and you will find that they will give you the information you need. Watch your thoughts jealously and be sure to think only of what you want, not what you do not want.

Numbers in sequence have a specific meaning, these numbers have messages in three dimensions, and guide us in our lives.

When you learn to interpret these numbers, you will feel more connected to the Angels, and this connection is the key that will open the door to peace, hope, and love.

Each number has vibrations that relate directly to their meanings and the Angels draw our attention to these number sequences because they feel devotion, and love for us. When you notice a number sequence, try to listen to what your Angel wants you to do or know.

The more you see these signs, the more frequently they will appear in your life. When you understand the meanings of these numbers and accept that they are not coincidences, but important, purposeful messages, you will learn to communicate with your Angels.

These number sequences can be birth dates, anniversaries, phone numbers or car license plates, and are a subtle reminder that something magical is happening in your life. It is up to you to go within, listen to your intuition and find out what the messages are telling you and what they mean to you.

How to Communicate with your Guardian Angel

Each of us, before we are born, is assigned to his guardian angel. They act through people's senses and imagination, but they can never act against the human will.

Guardian Angels cannot interfere in the lives of humans unless they are asked to do so or are in imminent danger of death.

To communicate with your Guardian Angel, you must ask for her help. The most fashionable way to communicate with your Angel is through prayers, but you can achieve this by being attentive to the messages and synchronicities that occur after you ask for her help. You should pay attention to your dreams and look for their meaning, listen to your intuition when you sense something unusual.

To contact your guardian Angel, you must invoke him because in this way you send him a message of your intention to receive his help and advice.

Emotions can create interference and prevent effective communication. Meditation is the best vehicle for establishing contact with your Guardian Angel. The calmer your mind is, the better you will be able to perceive your Guardian Angel.

Intuition, or the sixth sense, is the most effective form of communication with your Guardian Angel. That is why people who have encounters with Angels always experience them in moments of anxiety because in those moments, the human being reacts according to his or her instinct. That opens a channel of communication and lets the love of the Guardian Angel flow.

Contacting your Guardian Angel is a process that will allow you to enjoy a miraculous life full of blessings.

Aries Predictions

This year 2024 indicates that love, new understanding, and passion await you. Unexpected wealth may come your way, giving you security in your financial life. But remember, you must embrace uncertainty and be open to unexpected changes in your life. You will have achievements and recognition in your professional life.

A bright future awaits you. It is advisable that you look within yourself and take advantage of the qualities you have had since childhood, remember that maturing does not mean abandoning your purest essence, but allowing it to grow with you. You will have the possibility of finding a job that connects better with your interests, and will stimulate your life in many aspects, besides the economic one.

Taurus Predictions

This year 2024 you will also be lucky in the material sphere, but you will have to make efforts to achieve everything you have desired.

You will receive much economic well-being and inner joy. You must be prepared to receive protection in the economic sphere, prosperity will appear in your life in such a way that material inconveniences will disappear. You will start a new life and you will also achieve spiritual abundance.

Some difficulties may arise to solve the problems, so you must be confident and self-confident because everything will be a test that you can overcome.

Your angel recommends that you stay away from conflictive situations and try to neutralize any criticism coming from work colleagues.

Maintain discipline, without neglecting the search for a job that gives you better conditions and a healthier environment. You will end the year with several proposals on the table, remember to ask for divine enlightenment to make the best decisions.

Predictions for Gemini

Love and security come to you this year. You will have a partner with stability and full of happiness.

Love and joy. The light of love is coming into your life, you just must be patient. Enjoy the stability and happiness that is on its way and that you should receive with open arms. Leave behind the feelings of loneliness and receive the pure love that is reserved for you. Your dreams are about to come true. Your wishes may not be fulfilled exactly as you wanted, but eventually the reward will be exactly what you expected.

Your angel warns about situations that can become amplified if you do not pay the necessary attention. Be especially careful of abdominal problems or discomfort, as they could even compromise reproductive organs. Attention in time will keep you in good health.

After a period in which your finances were rocked to the sway of the waves, this year stability will return to your life.

Predictions for Cancer

Do you remember how magical the world around you seemed to be in your childhood? The Angels ask you to restore this magical feeling for yourself by remembering the wonderful powers around you. The Angels really want to support you, to help you discard unnecessary anxiety to radiate joy and spontaneity like a child.

You will protect your freedom above any other value, despite the criticism of others or the possible discussions that may arise in this regard.

It is very possible that you will begin to feel more comfortable being alone than in companies that do not allow you to grow. Travel and long conversations with friends may give you the light to change partners or rethink the terms of the relationship.

It will be a year of testing, for only those who understand life in a freeway will stay, while those who do not will surely take different paths.

Predictions for Leo

You are not alone; the Guardian Angels want to tell you that they will never leave you. Nothing you thought, said or did, can repel your divine assistants.

Remain calm in your daily life situations, as this year you may continue to experience insomnia. Do not try to embrace more than your strength can resist and you will witness positive changes in your physical and mental health.

Your economy will have momentous changes during this 2024. You should distance yourself from people who, with their attitude, take energy away from you instead of giving it to you. Do not be afraid of novelty, remember that your angel will be willing to help you get a new job in an optimal and accelerated way.

Your angel recommends you concentrate on your work and leave aside the competitiveness of your sign, because all that flow of energy will result in masterpieces if you concentrate.

Your personal brilliance will be unmistakable, sentimental possibilities will multiply, that is why your angels recommend you to be prudent and avoid temptations to focus your energy on the right way.

Virgo Predictions

This year you should choose a profession that you love. The Angels help you to find these talents in you.

Be prepared for unexplainable events and make the most of every opportunity. Wise Angels offer you to get rid of the habit that keeps you from moving forward. Do a variety of things and observe your life with interest. If the path ahead is complicated, function as if you are exploring an unknown place. Angels inspire you, move forward with expectation and hope.

You will have the possibility of creating your sentimental destiny, leaving doubts aside and taking a little more risk.

Keep the necessary precautions since an encouragement or award will make many people envy your triumphs. Your angel recommends reinforcing your self-esteem and recognizing that you are a being full of gifts and deserve the best that the universe can give you.

If you have a stable partner, the end of the year will be a very propitious time to advance in commitments that tend to the union between family groups and reorganization. Large investments supported by your partner will have successful results.

Libra Predictions

It is especially important for you this year 2024. You must meditate more often. To do this, when you wake up in the morning, stay in bed for the first five minutes with your eyes closed and breathe deeply. Talk to them and then listen carefully, what message will be sent to you.

The Angels tell you to stay away from all activities that do not reflect your intentions.

All issues related to your work, relationships, health, will be resolved surprisingly and successfully. Angels will constantly lead you to actions leading to corrections of any negative situation.

Your angel will show you the way to reconciliation with those you have left aside and will remind you that it is a bad idea to separate from those who have shown you constant fidelity.

Some allergies and throat problems may occur.

Your angel will activate your social life to unsuspected limits. Keep a relaxed pace and avoid very demanding exercises.

Scorpio Predictions

This year 2024 you must trust your intuition. This is what the Angels are telling you. The intuitive feelings you feel, the visions, the inner voice, all are attempts to tell you something important, so you must trust and follow these guidelines.

Remember that when you are asked to wait, it means that you have something better than you could ever imagine, prepared just for you. That is why you must change your attitude and accept the situation. Relax.

Ask your Angel to support you throughout this year so that you can listen to divine advice. Do not rush when you see something that may break your will. The next door will open when the time comes, and you will gain new strength.

Angels will help you meet your romantic needs. Ask for their help and accept it. Angels will help you look for the love of your life, they will guide you, telling you the way to fulfill your desires. For example, you may feel an ardent desire to go to a specific place. There you will meet a person with whom you will connect in a love affair.

The Angels also want you to improve your education.

Predictions for Sagittarius

A new chapter begins in your life. You will have a new partner, or an old relationship will be restored. Open your heart to that new feeling of love that will come to you.

Look closely at the people you meet on your path, be open to change in existing relationships and do not get too attached to your old ideas about them. There is a time of wonderful change in your life, so trust the Angels.

Some changes in your life can be painful if you do not show enough flexibility in your thoughts and actions. If you have a new love, remember that the past must remain in the past, away from the new happiness.

Your current relationship may end, or, on the contrary, move into a new phase of renewed love, the Angels ask you to trust them and follow their instructions.

If you already have a close relationship with a person, the Angels are asking you to give them a chance and decide what to do with them, try to develop a next level or end it to make way for a new love. In both cases the Angels will be with you, helping you to choose the right path!

Predictions for Capricorn

It is time to educate yourself. The Angels advise you not to save your strength or time for this activity, but to read, listen and develop yourself.

During this year it is important to dedicate yourself to the acquisition of new knowledge, ideas, and skills. You will want to start learning and if you are currently studying, the Angels are asking you to continue your education.

Sometimes, in the process of acquiring new knowledge and skills, we have a desire to quickly evaluate them in practice, and this leads to the fact that many people drop out of school early, the Angels advise you not to rush things. Continue your education.

The personal growth that accompanies learning can bring you joy if you remember the need in your thoughts to stay here and now.

Ask your angels to help you get rid of the fear of poverty, so you can fully enjoy the growth of abundance. Angels report the influx of abundance in your life. in your life. Continue to believe, this will provide you with constant material, emotional, spiritual, and intellectual support.

Aquarius Predictions

This year relax, grant the Angels a chance to help you. Whatever you give up will be replaced by something better.

You are behaving stubbornly that does not bring you anything good and does not allow happiness and health to enter your life.

If you are unhappy in love, if you are not advancing in your career, have family or financial problems, as well as illness, let the Angels adjust the situation.

If you stubbornly dwell on unfruitful aspects of your life, and fear that things will get worse, they really will. However, if you are willing to free yourself from the situation that oppresses you, the current situation will improve in a wonderful way.

The Angels ask you not to try to control the outcome of your current negative situation. Let it go.

The Angels confirm that, through your own feelings, dreams, visions, and intuition, you really hear them, and these are not hallucinations. If you suddenly have the desire to call someone, go somewhere, read something, it is important that you follow these inner impulses, the Angels ask you to abandon all doubts about divine guidance.

Predictions for Pisces

The Angels know of your past disappointments that have undermined your faith in yourself, others and even the Angels, yet they remind you of the importance of preserving your faith.

The Angels know that you, like everyone else, have made mistakes in the past. These mistakes, however, do not change your true nature. Within you, there is part of the divine nature, which is infallible. The Angels ask you to believe in yourself. Try to make sure that your thoughts and feelings reflect your true intentions.

The Angels ask you to choose your goals carefully and accomplish them with love. Visualize yourself in other happy, successful, and peaceful people. By sticking to highly spiritual intentions, you help yourself and others. The Angels ask you to replace negative thought habits with positive ones, just ask for their help.

Angelic Cards for each Zodiac Sign 2024

Aries. Zadquiel Angel Card

Zadquiel *is the Angel of mercy; he symbolizes altruism and personal selflessness in favor of others. Zadquiel will help you to be a compassionate person. He will help you find lost objects, improve your memory, and help you heal physically, emotionally, and mentally. Zadquiel will support you as you learn to forgive yourself and others, remember valuable information and study. If you want to leave behind any prejudice*

invoke the Archangel Zadquiel because one of his main tasks is to help you see your inner light.

You will stop seeing your mistakes as negative aspects of your life and start seeing them to learn. You will also see your flaws as blessings in your life because perfection is impossible to achieve and even in chaos there is beauty.

You will look for ways to focus on becoming the best version of yourself, the best person you can imagine. Archangel Zadquiel is a higher being that you can invoke when you feel frustration, sadness, or negativity. His armies can help you find the positive side of all situations and make you feel better emotionally.

It is time to let go of any guilt you cling to regarding mistakes you may have made in the past. Give yourself credit for doing your best, even if the results were not what you would have liked. Focus on the changes you have made that have made you a better person.

Taurus. Angelic Card Uriel

Uriel, *the Angel of the keys warns you to embark on new paths and to beware of bad influences. If you are beginning to doubt yourself, or losing faith, this card reminds you that all things are possible through learning. Knowledge can open all doors, and new skills can open all locks. The flame of knowledge never dies and is within your reach.*

Uriel will never lead you down an uncertain path without reason. He is there to support you along your journey, allowing you to speak your truth and become the best version of yourself.

This card reminds you that you are wiser than you think, and your inner wisdom will give you all the answers you seek. Embrace this knowledge and trust it. If you have doubts, ask it to give you obvious signs to validate your ideas.

Uriel helps to illuminate cloudy situations. However, he only illuminates one step at a time, so you may not be able to clearly discern the result of your actions. You must trust because you will know what step to take next, along the way, with Uriel's help.

Never forget that forgiveness can work miracles. When you release the past, a weight is lifted off your shoulders and a sense of freedom comes over you. Ask Uriel to help you relieve sadness or pain caused by others so you can be free.

Gemini. Raphael Angel Card

It represents strength and personal brilliance.

You must harness your personality to achieve success. Raphael's most powerful gift is his ability to transform lives through a cascade of positive energy. You can access this channel of energy through affirmations or meditation techniques. Throughout history, Raphael has had various appearances in many different religions, making him an Archangel accessible to people of all faiths.

Now is not the time to give up on sick relationships. There is still hope for the future.

Substantial changes will come into your life. You may find yourself on a new career path, entering a new relationship, or moving to a new house or city. Embrace these exciting events, Raphael will be by your side all the way.

Remember, the future is always changing. If you do not like the outcome, this is your opportunity to make changes that will alter it. If you like this outcome, stay on your current path. To maintain your current path, keep doing what you are doing. Take it easy or change the intensity with which you are currently working.

Rafael will help you recognize the ramifications of your actions and your purpose in life.

Cancer. Haniel Angel Card

It represents all the good that the earth offers us. A new successful stage will be presented in your life.

Haniel may be asking you to slow down and really think about the action you plan to take.

Haniel is trying to guide you to a higher choice, so put aside everything you think you know about your current circumstances or situation and simply allow the Universe and Haniel to point the way.

When it is necessary to make a weighty decision, this Angel will send you many signals through synchronicity as to which is the right path to take.

It is important that you take some time to regroup, as this Angel may come to give you the guidance you need at that moment.

This letter has appeared to bring you messages of hope, as well as to indicate that it is time for you to start being more aware of all the messages that the Universe and Haniel are sending you.

You may need some answers to some tough questions, or you may have been wondering if things will ever get better in your life. Haniel has appeared to say that they will, however, think carefully about what you say to others and what they say to you. Haniel will never judge you for anything you think or say, however, he will urge you to focus on those things that bring you a sense of joy, peace, and gratitude.

Leo. Gabriel Angel Card

Gabriel shows you the duality of good and bad. He augurs travel for you,
 You may begin to have some thoughts in your mind that will surprise you. It is important for you to keep in mind that the stronger your emotional reaction to them, the more you should pay attention to them. Notice what others tell you that fits with what you have been thinking. When you ask Gabriel to confirm that what you have been thinking is true, he is always quick to act, so pay attention.

You may feel inclined to spend time meditating or reading self-help books. Gabriel is encouraging you to do so, because he knows how important it is to fill your mind with positive thoughts.

Gabriel allows you to understand that as you make changes in your life and face challenges, you are in complete safety. He knows what will be best for you. Remember that when you are asked to wait, it means that you have something better than you could ever imagine, prepared just for you. That is why you must accept the situation.

Do not rush when you see something that may break your will. The next door will open when the time comes, and you will have new strength.

Virgo. Remiel Angel Card

Remiel represents the mercy of God showing that something has been hidden from you. During this year 2024 it is important to dedicate yourself to acquiring new knowledge, ideas, and skills. You will want to start learning and this card encourages you to follow this desire.

If you are currently studying, Remiel asks you to continue your education. Sometimes, in the process of acquiring new knowledge and skills, we have a desire to quickly evaluate them in practice, and this leads to the fact that many people drop out of school early.

This card advises you not to rush things. Continue your education. The personal growth that accompanies learning can bring you joy.

Remiel knows that you have many responsibilities in life, so you need time, money, and other resources. This card wants to remind you that regular doses of entertainment can help you achieve your goals. Have fun and laugh, relax. In this state, you become more receptive to innovative ideas, spiritual links, teachings, and divine energy.

In addition, your cheerfulness attracts to you many wonderful people who can help you. Your cheerful outlook toward the world opens new opportunities for you.

Libra. St. Michael Angel Card

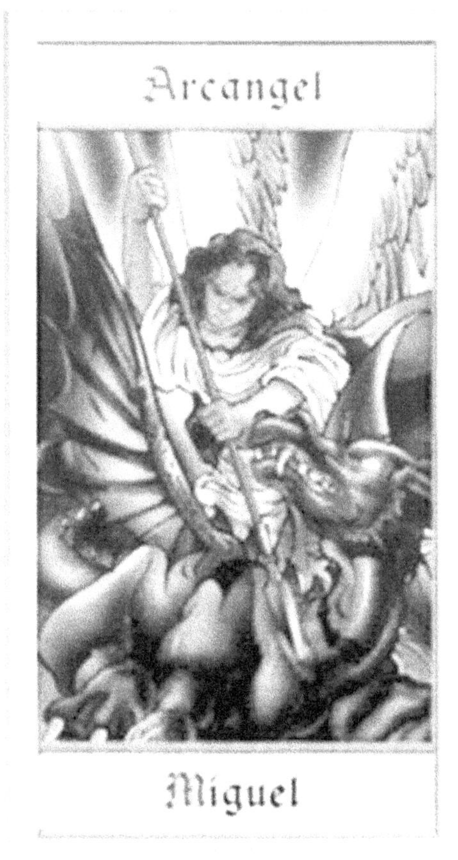

Archangel Michael represents justice, and the forces of good prevailing over evil.

You do not have to forgive mistakes, but if you forgive a person, you will find peace. You have many negative emotions and Michael calls you to cleanse your soul, he understands that these feelings can be completely justified, but he asks you to see the high price you are paying for accumulating all this anger.

Get rid of all the pain and anger of the past. When you forgive yourself and others, your karma is cleansed of the burden of past mistakes.

All the power of the creator is within you. All the power of divine love and wisdom is at your disposal. You can see the angels and the future, and you also have the intelligence to know the universal wisdom of the divine mind.

Thanks to your emotional power, you will be able to confront other people and your psychic power will be truly infinite during 2024. The angels ask you to eliminate all fears associated with the use of force. They see your true power radiating from Divine Love. Allow yourself to shine with this love so that your true power can accomplish the miracles you need.

Sometimes you may think that you are a hostage to life's circumstances, but this card asks you to understand that you are your own prisoner. Once you know you can break free, you will be free immediately.

Everything you do in your life; you do by your choice. Even prisoners are free to choose their thoughts, and, therefore, can find peace and happiness under any circumstances. The next time you start a sentence with the words "I am forced...", stop. Ask Michael to show you alternatives. He will help you.

Scorpion. Raziel Angelic Card

He is the Angel of secrets and mysteries. He will reveal to you in 2024 mysteries of the earthly and spiritual realm.

A period of spiritual growth begins in your life this year, and although you will experience mixed feelings of confusion, fear, and surprises, you must not lose your cool. Discard your fears. Raziel supports you, loves you and guides you every second. Do not worry about how your future will harmonize with your growth.

You will get important messages in your dreams. There is a time of wonderful changes in your life, so trust Raziel, he will take care of exactly what you want.

Changes in your life can be painful if you do not show flexibility in your thoughts. If you have a new love, remember that the past remains in the past, away from the new happiness.

You need to expand your horizons, and Raziel is here to help you. It is time to listen to your heart. Be aware of the importance of tact and do not be too stubborn. Trust yourself. Do not worry. Whatever challenge you face, you are on your way to serenity.

You need comfort and this angel gives you faith. Soon you may be on the road to the happiness and harmony you need. Do charitable deeds, it will help you feel better, and you will receive good things in return.

Sagittarius. Metatron Angel Card

It represents the greatness and strength that a person should have. By inviting Metatron into your life, you open yourself to receive spiritual and energetic healing, to cleanse yourself of all negativities. You get protection from illness and, of course, you get closer to transformation.

You need to honor all the emotions you are feeling right now whether they are good or bad. Emotions can teach us a lot about our true feelings and the people or situations that evoked them.

You may be getting feedback from other people, and this is the mirror for you to see what is inside.

Metatron protects you by cutting the cords that bind you to people, places, and things. If you are afraid, lack courage or need protection, imagine his protective mantle around you, helping you to live your truth. This is a special card. You are guided and sustained. Metatron is with you currently, and there is a special message he wants to share with you. Close your eyes, take a few deep breaths, go deep within, and relax. Listen to the advice you receive.

You are perfect, and that is a spiritual fact. Metatron gently embraces you and lets you know that you are the perfect spiritual being. You are not alone, no matter how you feel. Place all your worries in his hands and allow him to heal your problems through divine guidance.

Your life has meaning, and every step is an essential part of your journey but rest assured that you are always protected and that all the angels are watching you with great love. Trust.

Capricorn. Raguel Angel Card

He is the Angel who gives advice to men to guide them on their path in life.

Your soul mate will come into your life. If you are free, consider the card as a sign from Raguel that your soul mate is present.

Suppose you are currently in a relationship, and you know that it is not your soul mate. In that case, you and your partner will be gently guided to improve the relationship, or to a graceful end, to obtain a new relationship with your soul mate.

Focusing better on your heart's desires and better contact with your higher self will help you complete all the troublesome work and issues you have put off. You have a list of goals for this year 2024 you should clear your mind and focus your thoughts better on what you really want, and you will be able to achieve your desires.

Visualizing your wishes is the fastest way to open the door to the universe and its offer to fulfill them. Do not worry about how your wishes will come to you. Leave it in the hands of the universe.

Listen to your higher self and ask the angels to guide you. Start acting as soon as you feel encouraged. Sometimes the results may not be what you expected, but that is the beauty of life and the universe. You are guided to what you really need.

Aquarius. Amiel Angel Card

It heralds changes you will have to adapt to and unexplored terrain you will visit.

Allow yourself to spend quality time with your family and friends. You can draw a lot of strength from those who love you. If you have a problem with a family member or friend, Amiel encourages you to bring it to the surface.

Releasing and healing will set you free, which will create more favorable opportunities for you. Or a simple act of spending quality time with your loved ones will yield positive results.

As you advance spiritually, you will become more sensitive to the dense, negative vibrations of reality along with the higher dimensions of love. This card is an encouragement to clear your energetic space.

This year take a relaxed breath and imagine that you are surrounded by an orb of white light. Amiel brings you blessings.

Your prayers will be heard and answered. Love, finances, friendship, and family will be determined by your attitude. Ask Amiel to help you treat yourself with the respect you so richly deserve. When you are in this state of self-esteem, you are full of positive energy that overflows to the people around you. This enables you to attract positive and loving relationships that are fulfilling.

Pisces. Dobiel Angel Card

Messenger of divine secrets.

Whether angels, family, neighbors, or friends, you will receive help. By asking for help, you are allowing the universe to act on your behalf. Believe that you will be led to the right person or situation that can help you in any matter.

We are not islands unto ourselves, and we are not obligated to solve all problems independently. Angels love to share, and a shared problem is half the

*problem. Never be afraid to ask for help. Miracles
exist and you are entitled to them.*

Numerology 2024

There is no such thing as chance, there is synchronicity. We are all born on a day, place, date, and time that are not a whim of fate. We bring specific missions and lessons from past lives.

By using numerology, we will have more autonomy and take control of our destiny.

Numerology is the study of numbers and their meaning. It is a discipline based on the concept that the name, day, month, and year of your birth contain fundamental information related to you. By analyzing the numerical values of the letters that make up your first and last name and the digits in your birth date, you can learn important aspects of your personality and your purpose in life.

Numerology is an ancient esoteric tradition that has been used by all mystics and philosophers for thousands of years in China, Greece, Rome, and Egypt.

Numerology is the correspondence between numbers and events, and the analysis of how they affect life. We can use Numerology to know ourselves and explore our talents. It is so broad that we can use it to acquire information about our health, professions, relationships, and purposes in life.

Numerology 2024

*According to Numerology 2024 this year adds the number **8**.*

This number is related to abundance, power, balance, and justice.

During this 2024 we must reevaluate the way we relate to prosperity. We must be organized, pay our financial debts, and organize our lives more efficiently. It is a year where we must value our time and focus on the important things.

We must learn to live without fear, and we must try to heal our wounds on a subconscious level.

This year will give you the opportunity to be prosperous on a spiritual and material level. You must raise your self-esteem levels to achieve it.

It will be a year with many challenges, but you must remember that you will learn from them.

Worldwide there will be an increase in criticism and rebellions against abuses, tyrannies, violence, and dictatorships.

What does the number 2024 mean spiritually?

*The meanings of the individual digits that make up the
number 2024 according to numerology are:*
The number 2 *symbolizes duality, family, private and
social life. You will enjoy your home life and family
gatherings.*

*The number 2 indicates a sociable, friendly, and
empathetic person. It is the number of cooperation,
adaptability, and consideration for others.*

*This number symbolizes balance, union, and affinity. It
is also an excellent mediator, honest and diplomatic. It
represents intuition and vulnerability.*

The number 4 *comes to establish stability and evokes
the sense of duty and discipline. It speaks to us of
building solid foundations. This number teaches you to
evolve in the material world, and to develop your
logical mind.*

The number 0 *everything begins at the zero degree
and at the zero point it ends. Sometimes we do not
know the end, but we perceive the beginning, that is
the zero point.*

Tarot card according to the numerology 2024

The Strength.

Strength is the Tarot card 11 and 8 at the same time.
This tarot card symbolizes firmness, strength, and
tenacity to survive.

This arcanum represents the ability to overcome
obstacles. The power of intelligence over strength. It is

also the representation of patience, intuition, and reconciliation of opposites.

From the astrological point of view, the arcane of The Strength of the Tarot is related to the zodiac sign Leo and the planet Mars.

This tarot card numerologically has two perspectives, since it is number 11 in the Tarot de Marseille, a master number, and number 8 in the Rider Waite Tarot.

The Strength is the prototype of endurance. Always in touch with his intuition and creativity, but with a super-developed talent, liveliness, perception, and subtlety.

The Strength has the capacity to control the most essential instincts to achieve its purposes. It never surrenders, and it does not die out, it only resists.

The Strength unfailingly achieves what it sets out to do, overcoming every difficulty with perspicacity and cunning.

This arcane will test your capacity for endurance, fortitude, tolerance, your limits, and if you really want to change something, or achieve a goal, you will have to be persevering without giving up trying.

This means that to achieve your goals you will have to stop being impatient, banish fear, and bury your ego.

If last year you were trying to reach a goal and you couldn't reach it that means you were using the wrong methods. So, this year The Strength is asking you not to change the goal, but to change your attitude and the methods that are not working for you.

You must use the energies of the arcane The Strength to fill yourself with its courage and endurance. You must be stoic, daring, and determined, to conquer your fears, and you will achieve this only with discipline and perseverance.

Nothing will prevent you from reaching your goals, you should not rush, nor should you turn your back on the challenges that come your way.

This is an arcane of power, do not rush, embrace the challenges, and continue patiently. You possess the power and endurance to win. Don't feel bad about things that are out of your control, focus on you, on your inner self. You must polish yourself to become your best version.

In love, this tarot card signifies fidelity and stable relationships. It symbolizes the daily effort that every couple must make to maintain a healthy relationship, so that it becomes a happy union.

In the material aspect this tarot card announces that a prosperous season is coming, and that if you are smart you will be able to master any situation no matter how difficult it may be. You will receive all the recognition you deserve; you will be rewarded. This is the year to fulfill your dreams.

Your work capacity will increase, you will be persevering, and you will know how to plan and go the extra mile, always with your eyes on the future.

This tarot card announces that your health will be good, as you will have a lot of vitality. You will have to be disciplined around your well-being, but you are on the right track, you will be very healthy.

This Tarot card: **The Strength,** *reminds you that you have the capacity and inner strength to be able to achieve everything you set your mind to.*

Definition of the Personal Year

Probably every time a year begins you ask yourself questions and write down goals without knowing what challenges the new year holds for you.

When a year begins, a chapter in our lives closes, but a cycle begins that challenges us because we are not sure if all our dreams can come true.

What's in store for me in the New Year? Will I buy a house, get a new partner, change jobs? Is this the right year to have children?

It is important to have an open mind when we are so uncertain about things that are new or different. But with numerology we can use our personal year and get an idea of how things may be.

The Universal Year Numbers are different from the others, because they do not depend on your name and date of birth. The first two digits of the Year Number represent the balance of that century. The third digit of the Year Number symbolizes the rhythm of the decade. The fourth digit has no specific meaning.

How to calculate your Personal Year.

This is an example:

Juan Carlos was born on December 7, 1965.

To know your personal year 2024, we make this calculation:

7 (day of birth) + 1+2 (month of birth) + 2 + 0 + 2 + 2 + 4(starting year) = 18 (1 + 8) = 9

For Juan Carlos, the year 2024 is a Personal Year 9.

This number is important, specifically if the result is one of the master numbers: 11, 22, 33.

The personal year describes what you must do during this period. They will be options, changes, or reinforcements that will enrich your path.

Personal Year 1

Key words for Year 1*: Transformation, Research, Engagement.*

A new chapter in your life begins. You're likely to move, get a new job or meet new people who will change your life forever.

This year you will lay the groundwork for new projects and ideas. It is a stage where you will be reborn. You should consider this year as the perfect time to change different aspects of your life, there are things that no longer work for you, and you must let them go.

This year offers you the invitation to take courage and try to fulfill your dreams, you will really have enthusiasm to make changes. Take courage and explore new opportunities and attitudes that will help you change the focus of your life.

This year 2024 is a personal invitation to trust, reflect on what you want, choose objectively, and decide what you want to succeed in. Try to choose what really makes you happy.

Start by cataloging the things you want to change, including improvements in your daily life, such as changing your eating habits or exercising. Remember that to start something you must plan it with consistency and determination.

This year is the perfect opportunity to close a cycle, you must leave behind everything that is not useful to you. Concentrate on what will help you grow, develop, or learn. Do not be afraid to let go of what was useful in the past.

You need to forget the past and look to the future. Too many things have happened that may have confused your mind, those things prevent you from accessing the paths that lead to happiness.

If you have businesses and projects, strive to keep them growing without forcing things. Try to give everything a rhythm.

Try not to acquire new debts.

Life will reward you.

Personal Year 2

Key words for Year 2: *Responsibility, Harmony, Stability.*

This year you should continue to build. The year 2024 will allow you to meet tutors, teachers, or even a partner. The energies of the year focus on cooperation and patience.

You start a development phase, and you must put your initiatives into practice. This year 2 may seem slow, but it is a period of defining your objectives.

You will probably encounter obstacles or people who try to limit your path, so it is important not to get overwhelmed and anxious. You should not worry about the things that are hindering your initiatives, it is just the natural settling in, and it is part of your growth process.

You must learn to be more diplomatic and tactful. People may appear willing to distract you, but that should not limit you from making new friends.

If when you did the calculation, the sum was 11, it means that you have reached your moment to breathe, to evolve and to become conscious.

The year of blessings is upon you. Try to get rid of all toxic people if you want to have a prosperous year, do not trust anyone.

The year 2024 offers you the opportunity to let go of your past worries and take charge of your life with more enthusiasm.

Life will present you with completely new plans and give you the opportunity to build your future if you leave the past behind. It is the year to think about yourself, break limits and not self-sabotage.

You must have courage and face life from a positive approach.

Personal Year 3

Key words for Year 3*: Agility, Creativity, Information.*

This is the year for you to look for ways to share your wisdom with the world. You will feel part of a greater whole and you will have much satisfaction and fulfillment.

You need to get rid of the feelings of restriction that you have accumulated. The only way to get results this year is to allow your creativity to express itself. Let go of rigidity, let your imagination be free. You must go the extra mile.

Find a new hobby, change your habits, start implementing new ideas and solutions to the challenges you face along the way.

You will have to work very hard, but you could strengthen your individual bonds, and form more formal relationships. These ties will be tested, certain relationships do not suit you. Perhaps they give you a lot of fun but have a dark side. Try to establish common goals with the people you love.

During this year you should be more conscious with your nutrition, and rest as your energy levels will be low.

Personal Year 4

Key words for Year 4: *Renewal, Restoration, Innovation, Assertiveness.*

This year you must work hard and be organized. If you manage to stay in the present, you can get to where you want to be.

Now is the time for you to reflect and analyze your personal goals. You need to establish a plan so that you can achieve something specific and well-structured.
Try to think about your future, try to assume all responsibilities and organize all your projects carefully.

You may be a little self-critical and this may result in you establishing your views strongly, being more determined and fighting.

This is positive as it will allow you to notice all the changes that occur in your environment.

All the above will inevitably have a positive effect on your family relationships and close friendships. you will be more assertive, and this will have a positive impact on your personal relationships.

If you organize yourself, this will be a year of prosperity, abundance, and triumphs. Trust in yourself because you will be able to recover your enthusiasm and live with illusion.

Inertia is your worst enemy this year, as well as negative thoughts.

Destiny offers you the opportunity to achieve everything you yearn for, dare to fight for those dreams.

Personal Year 5

Key words for Year 5*: Character, Will, Effort, Courage, Courage, Ratification, Recognition, Visualization.*

A year where you will enjoy many adventures, emotions and where you will have the opportunity to plant seeds with the intention to succeed.

Year 5 for you is like an injection of enthusiasm, plan because it is a year of many changes. You must be prepared for some unforeseen circumstances. Try to be receptive to all opportunities and to all challenges.

You must have mental clarity, be cautious and never underestimate your potential.

Try to expand your circle of friends, keep your public image healthy, and pay close attention to the contracts you must sign.

Take care of yourself because this way you will have the success you deserve. Establish habits that will allow you to ensure your prosperity for years to come. Calculate the risks and decide on the perfect opportunities when they present themselves to you.

Don't rush and act wisely, always thinking about what is best for you in the long term. Forget about immediate results and accept that things take time, and you can't always expect them to happen when you want them to.

Personal Year 6

Key words for Year 6*: Reorganize, Reborn Reform, Replace, Manifest, Disseminate, Transmit, Inform, Participate.*

This year 2024 offers you the opportunity to heal sentimental wounds and to free yourself from all the repressed emotions that sleep in your subconscious.

You will be very focused on your home and family. It is the perfect time to create a more stable and harmonious environment in your surroundings.

It is key that this year you learn to share all that you have received in abundance. It is also necessary that you avoid impulsive actions so that you do not make mistakes.

Always act ethically, try to stay calm and be confident in your decisions. You will see incredible results and it will all be thanks to your courage. Everything that was paralyzed will suddenly begin to flow and you will feel liberated. Perhaps in some periods you will notice instability, but this is necessary for you to break the routine.
You will have opportunities to travel, enjoy and control excesses of any kind.

Personal Year 7

Key words for Year 7*: Investigation, Observation, Verification, Control, Transformations, Metamorphosis.*

During this year you will have many changes. These changes may be related to your friendships, relationships, work, and home.
There is a possibility that you will meet someone important who will help you advance in your profession or perhaps you will become engaged.

This is a "parenthesis" year as you will stop to value everything you have done. You must let go of everything that is not working, be it objects or relationships.
For this you must perfect your analytical skills and not be afraid to calmly make a thorough review of what limits you.

Due to these purification processes, your relationships will be debated. Through comparison you eliminate mistakes and errors.

You will be attracted to esoteric subjects, but you will grow spiritually. Don't forget that everyone comes to this life with a different contract than you and that you should not judge the path of others. Everyone is where he or she is meant to be.

Personal Year 8

***Keywords for Year 8:** Success, Evolution, Restoration, Transformation, Rehabilitation, Reconstruction, Prosperity.*

Much abundance and success on your way. You will feel blessed by all the opportunities that will come your way. This personal year is related to karma, so if you have acted well, dividends await you. It will be an important year where you will be very busy.

This year you must put each piece in its place. It is time to make decisions, reflect, and choose what and who you want for your life.

You will feel more confident and will have more mental capacity to face challenges. You should take risks and begin studies that will help you to advance in your profession.
You will want to enjoy moments of solitude, accompanied by your thoughts, far away from the hustle and bustle of social networks. You should practice meditation combined with breathing techniques.
Do not give so much importance to superfluous matters, and toxic people.

Personal Year 9

Key words for Year 9: Overcome, Finish, Conclude, Accomplish, Perceive, Perceive, be instructed, be trained, Study, Experience, Deepen.

This year will be difficult if you resist change. It is a year of endings. Throw out what is useless and stay away from energy vampires.

Surround yourself with people who bring you knowledge and good energy. Protect yourself from black magic. Organize your house, throw away what you do not use, broken things, because in this way you will be making space for the new.

You must decide what you really want to do in your life, destiny will scream in your ears what you really want and if you are willing to fight for it.

The commitment this year is with yourself, you must. give up your fears and insecurities because during this period you should be attentive and not complain so much.

Your Soul Number. How to calculate it

Your soul number manifests your desires, satisfactions, hobbies, concerns, worries, and discomforts.

The soul is the spiritual part that we all have. Together with the mind and the body, the soul makes up the human being. In numerology, the soul is related to a number called: soul number.

This number comes from the vowels of the birth name and represents the inner self.

If you wish to calculate your soul number, you must identify the vowels of your full name. Do not forget to include middle names.

*You must use the vowels **A, E, I, O** U. If by chance your name has a Y, since the Y performs the function of a vowel you must use it. Examples are the names: Daryl, Dylan, Henry,* **and** *Taylor.*

The numerical value of each vowel is as follows:
A = 1
E = 5
I = 9
O = 6
U = 3
Y = 7

When you have identified the number of each vowel in your full name, the next step is to add them all up and reduce them to a single digit, except for the numbers 11 or 22, which are master numbers.

Meaning of the Soul Number

Number 1:
Independent souls who can take good care of themselves, have a clear vision of life goals and purposes.

Number 2:
Loving, artistic, calm, peaceful and polite, these are the soul's number 2. They also have a great imagination and creativity.

Number 3:
They are strong, determined, courageous, compassionate, enthusiastic, and very optimistic. They constantly think about the future.

Number 4:
They are obsessed with order, stability, and control. They are often frustrated when things don't go according to plan.

Number 5:

They are free, traveling souls who enjoy meeting new people. Challenges excite them and they are considered a leader soul.

Number 6:

Love is their most powerful soul, so they tend to prioritize the interests of others over their own. They are very balanced and full of harmony.

Number 7:

They live in a constant mental analysis of what they want from the world and life in general. They are very talented artists and not at all ambitious.

Number 8:

They are leading souls or figures in society, they aspire to be rich and have power and high status. Their ambition makes them the best at what they do. Number 9: It is the most selfless and dreamy soul. It is charismatic, understanding, and makes the world a better place.

Number 11:

They are creative, artistic, and charismatic. They possess a psychic side due to being one of the most sensitive souls.

Number 22:

It is a soul closely related to the 4 (2+2=4), but adds the characteristics of honesty, kindness, and attention to detail.

How to Calculate your Personal House Number

Your house number offers you the secrets to take advantage of its energetic vibrations. The home is our sanctuary, where our dreams, our family, and our ideas live. All these things are our treasures, that's why we must take care of the energetic flow that surrounds us, specifically inside our home.

The decoration, the colors with which we paint our house influence the harmony, but they are not the only ones to consider. The address of your house offers predictive information according to numerology.

Steps to Calculate your Personal House Number

To know your personal home number, you must add up all the numbers that make up your address until you have a single digit.

Example**: If you live in the number 2550, you must add **2+5+5+5+0= 12
1+2= 3

If your address has letters included, you must look in the alphabetical table and change those letters to numbers.

1 (A, J, S)
2 (B, K, T)
3 (C, L, U)
4 (D, M, V)
5 (E, N, W)
6 (F, O, X)
7 (G, P, Y)
8 (H, Q, Z)
9 (I, R)

If you lived in a building with the number 2550, in apartment 8F, you must add up all the numbers and letters.

Example: **2+5+5+0+8+6 (6 is the letter F) = 26**
2+6=8.

The 8 will be the number that corresponds to this house.
Remember that if there were letters in the address it would be another number because you would have to add those numerical values to the previous one.

Meaning of your House number

Number 1

You must be very attentive to the type of energies that enter your house because the people who visit you leave bad energies inside your home. With neighbors you should be careful because they are very envious, they are curious about who enters and leaves your house, and those bad eyes create an energetic imbalance.

Number 2

It indicates that the happiness of your house does not lie in its luxury, but in the harmony that you are able to maintain inside it. This house will make you forget the chaos that exists in the world. The way you communicate, the words you say are important because houses are containers of energies. Everything is engraved on the walls. There is the possibility of accidents inside.

Number 3

*This house number means enthusiasm, optimism, happiness. In these houses the energy is in constant movement. In this house you will be able to achieve your goals and be successful. **The number** 3 attracts* *good luck, for that reason in this house people will always be undertaking new projects.*

Number 4

If your house has this number, you will not live in it for long, let's say it is a transit house. It is a house for new beginnings, here you can start your family, but guaranteed that when it grows you will move. If you stay here for a long time, discrepancies, disagreements, contradictions, antagonisms, hostilities, and inconsistencies will constantly arise.

Number 5

In this house there will always be parties or family gatherings. You may not have to do much structural work, but there will always be a lot of tension inside the house because of all the people who visit it. In this house there will never be two similar days. Its owners will be very diverse, but if you like it and you don't want to move, you must be constantly cleaning it energetically.

Number 6

This house always has good vibes, that's why you should keep it illuminated. It is the perfect home for newly married couples starting a life project. Here the family will have the necessary conditions to live in peace. It will also make the people who live here compassionate.

Number 7

This is the ideal house for artists as it has favorable conditions for creativity and reflection. Its inhabitants will be very spiritual. For writers and students, it would be the perfect one. It is advisable to check periodically if the house has escapes of energies or concentration of bad vibrations.

Number 8

This number is related to wealth; however, it is not the appropriate place to form and maintain a family, nor to live happily with your partner. **In this house everyone will be constantly concerned only with money and** *material* **things.** *This can create tension in the home. For a workplace it is perfect.*

Number 9

In this house people can become a bit dull and vague, although within this house there will be balance, fairness, equality, and empathy. This would be the ideal house for a social worker, or a lawyer. It possesses healing energies.

Birthday Number. Meaning

People with esoteric knowledge know that our soul chooses the day to be born into this world, and that we come with goals to achieve that are destined.

Your Birthday Number is the day you were born, and it has a very strong impact on your life. The Birthday Number identifies specific traits that will help you move forward in life.

By knowing your birthday number and its meaning, you can reduce or eliminate negative characteristics and refine positive ones.

How to Calculate Your Birthday Number

This is a simple calculation. You write the number on the date you were born and reduce it to a single digit if necessary. If you were born between the 1st and 9th of a month, you do not need to reduce the numbers. However, if your birthday was after the 10th of the month, you must reduce it until you reach a single digit.

Example:

If you were born on the 18th of the month, it would be 1 + 8 = 9.

Number of Birthdays 1

If you were born on the 1st, 10th, 19th or 28th of a month, your Birthday Number is 1.

This means that you have leadership skills and are very independent. You are creative and, you possess a lot of enthusiasm.

If you were born on the 1st of the month, *you are charming and have creative ways to complete your goals. Almost every innovator or pioneer in history has had 1 as their Birthday Number.*

You possess easy earning skills and are dynamic by nature. At times you appear aloof and give the impression that you are ignoring others or are brusque.

As you are a natural leader, you rarely rest, your energy is nervous. Personally, when it comes to relationships you are strong. You are honest, have strong willpower and think quickly.

If you were born on the 10th of the month, *you are intuitive and are most successful when you listen to your hunches. You are dynamic, idealistic, and able to inspire others.*

You have a unique ability to reinvent yourself when necessary, and because you are so creative you can succeed in any business.

You don't like to pay attention to details and prefer to work alone. In your personal life you relate to many people, but you call few of them friends.

If you were born on the 19th of the month, *you are competitive, strong-willed, and like to succeed. You have an incredible ability to create and start new businesses and you like to take risks.*

Being a leader comes very naturally to you, but you work best when you are alone. Sometimes you may feel lonely, even when you are with a group of people and find it difficult to reflect on others.

Your personality is magnetic, and you prefer to overcome challenges in peace. You rarely get upset, but when it happens you explode, although you never hold grudges.

***If you were born on the 28th of the month**, you are strong-willed, intelligent, and like to stand out. You are rebellious and do not like to follow rules as you are quite independent. You are very practical, but analytical and understand the basic concepts of humanity.*

You can apply logic to get the results you need. You are a perfectionist, but because you are innovative, you never fail.

Number of Birthdays 2

If you were born on the 2nd, 11th, 24th or 29th of the month, your Birthday Number is Number 2.

These people enjoy harmony and teamwork, but they are sensitive. They are very cooperative and enjoy the good things in life.

***If you were born on the 2nd of the month**, you often play tricks with life and multitask with ease. Deep down, you want to be at peace, achieving balance in your life is one of your resolutions.*

You are diplomatic, have an ambitious side and like to work in a team. On an emotional level, you take things too seriously and can sometimes underestimate yourself.

Those who are close to you are important in your life, since, in your search for happiness, you need family and friends around you so you should try to choose your relationships carefully.

Your home is very important, you take care of it and love to spend time at home.

***If you were born on the 11th of the month**, you are intuitive and enjoy hard work because this way you can transform your ideas into reality. You tend to be anxious; a balanced lifestyle is recommended for you.*

It is important that you get enough rest, as your energy levels can be depleted. You love being in contact with nature and surrounded by animals.

On an emotional level, you tend to get attached to the pain or disappointments of the past. You need to let go of the past; you need to work on your confidence levels so that you develop self-confidence.

***If you were born on the 20th** of the month, you are tactful and diplomatic. You try to adapt in life and fit into any group because of your empathy and your ability to feel at ease wherever you are.*

You are happiest when you are with people who are like you, you are emotional and sensitive, and you sometimes overindulge those around you.

Other people take advantage of your desire to help, so it is important that you have quality time alone so you can enjoy peace.

If you were born on the 29th *of the month you are very sensitive, but you enjoy sharing time with others. You have a very strong character, but you easily inspire others.*

You have natural leadership abilities. If you wish to succeed in your profession, you must choose one that utilizes your talents. You tend to shyness, but you can overcome it, even if you are in the spotlight because your personality is very strong.

You like money and power, but you are very generous with others. It is very important for you to stay on the straight and narrow instead of opting for easy routes. You tend to mood swings, so you must keep your emotions in balance.

Inside you there are many feelings of insecurity, although you long to be able to love deeply. You are reserved, hiding your feelings for fear of being ridiculed. There is a possibility that in your childhood you may have had a trauma, and this may persuade you to have children.

Number of Birthdays 3

If you were born on the 3rd, 12th, 21st or 30th of the month, you have an incredible sense of humor and are very creative. You are a good communicator, kind, enthusiastic and like to have fun.

If you were born on the 3rd of the month, *you easily excel in your creative abilities. Your communication skills are excellent, and you are very popular.*

Other people are attracted to you in every way. Sometimes you seem distant because people don't always understand you, but there are even times when you don't understand yourself.

You possess the ability to keep your mood from deteriorating and are a problem solver par excellence.

If you were born on the 12th of the month, *you are a child in your heart and soul. As you are a people person, people are attracted to you, and you will always have friends. You have deep feelings and are committed to the people you love. You sometimes hide your feelings and your needs from others. This can* *lead you to be a mysterious person. You have a good vocabulary and express yourself well, which makes you a master, so you could be a public speaker. You have many interests in different areas of life, but it is important that you do not take on so many responsibilities.*

If you are born on the 21st of the month *you attract luck and opportunities. You enjoy sharing your good fortune with others. You are very popular but reserved at social events. You can talk to anyone about anything and have a natural optimism for life.*

Your attitude helps others improve their mood, and although you are stubborn at times, you have a curious mind. There are times when you feel nervous because you are constantly on the move; rest is important to you.

If you were born on the 30th of the month, *you are very creative and entertain others naturally. You are charming and succeed in life thanks to your creativity. Occasionally you find it difficult to achieve your personal goals. When you have money, you are generous, you are attracted to the good things in life. People find it difficult to get to know your true personality even though you are super fun to be with.*

Number of Birthdays 4

If your birthday is on the 4th, 13th, 22nd or 31st of the month, your Birthday Number is 4.

With this Birthday Number, you possess a desire for security and a need to create solid structures for your future. You are self-disciplined, sincere, and fair.

If you were born on the 4th day of the month, *you are conventional and practical in your approach. You know how to get what you want in life and have the determination to do it.*

Sometimes your likes and dislikes are noticeable, and it is difficult for you to change your way of thinking. You are happy when you can enjoy life. It is important that you take time to increase your vitality. You should emphasize rest. In love it is very difficult for you to express your deepest emotions. You have appearances of seriousness, however, once people discover how kind you are, they adore you.

If you were born on the 13th of the month, *you are a complex person. You are intellectual and have a monumental capacity for reasoning. You have a talent for overcoming obstacles and can sense when things are going wrong to counteract them.*

You are a good problem solver and are practical and energetic in your approach. Traditions are important to you, as is your family.

You have a balanced attitude, but sometimes, you allow yourself to have fun.

***If you were born on the 22nd of the month**, you are a natural organizer and leader. You are curious and seek answers to life's riddles. Although you are independent, you work well with groups.*

You have a natural zest for life, and balance is important to you. Your moods can easily wane. You possess many unusual friendships and have a need to make them happy. At times, you are sensitive and try to hide your feelings to project that you are strong.

***If you were born on the 31st of the month**, you are always on the move and travel frequently. You have artistic gifts, but your mind is strong and determined. You have ideas, and the ability to harness these ideas and put them into practice if necessary. You are hardworking, practical and have an anchor in the ground. You have high ideals and are honest. At times, you can be rigid in your ways, so try to be flexible.*

Number of Birthdays 5

If you were born on the 5th, 14th or 23rd of the month, your Birthday Number is 5.

You have an exacerbated sense of adventure. Being free is important to you, but this makes you impatient. You enjoy change, are resourceful, curious, and an advanced thinker.

If you were born on the 5th of the month, *you are untraditional, and you like to do whatever you want. You have a unique outlook on life. Your energy is boundless, this means that you are in constant motion and can be rebellious because you hate to follow the rules. Your personality is magnetic, others find you fascinating. You have difficulty with commitment and are quick to analyze.*

If you were born on the 14th of the month, *you enjoy calculated risks, and this is part of your personality. You possess an excellent memory, which leads you to think about the pains of the past. You need to be flexible and adaptable. You enjoy food and drink; you indulge your senses too much. You are very generous, and others adore you.*

If you were born on the 23rd of the month, you are versatile and think very fast. You trust your intuition; you may have psychic abilities. You always listen to your inner voice, you possess a lot of energy, and this can unsettle you and lead you to experience new things. Although you face many challenges, you always land on your feet.

Number of Birthdays 6

If your birthday falls on the 6th, 15th or 24th, your Birthday Number will be 6.

You avoid arguments, preferring peace, and harmony in your environment. You often feel uneasy if you argue with others. People are attracted to your magnetism.

If you were born on the 6th of the month, you have business skills, you are artistic and charming. You can overcome any challenge. You give importance to your family life and always help those in need. You often take on too much responsibility.

You enjoy giving advice to others but find it difficult to accept criticism.

If you were born on the 15th of the month, you are sensitive. You are empathetic and will try to help those *in need. Sometimes you take on other people's problems and it can be very difficult for you to let them go. Family life is very important to you. You are very respected in business; you attract influential people into your life.*

***If you were born on the 24th of the month**, you work hard to achieve your goals, and you like to be simple. The key to your success is your practical and fair approach. You often take over when others can't keep up, but you expect others to take responsibility as well. You often find yourself surrounded by children, or by people with a jovial nature. Your home is your sanctuary and music are your favorite way to relax.*

Number of Birthdays 7

If you were born on the 7th, 16th and 25th of the month, your Birthday Number is 7.

You are reflective and are always looking for meaning in life. You take a measured approach when you must make decisions because you hate to make mistakes. You are attracted to nature because it nurtures your mind and soul.

***If you were born on the 7th of the month**, you have a distant appearance, because you possess a natural shyness. You love privacy and few people know the* *real you. You are very curious and are constantly asking questions, although you are reluctant to be questioned. You trust your intuition.*

If you were born on the 16th of the month, *your power of perception is excellent, you detect evil immediately. It is important that you finish what you started, for that you must be more analytical. You are often considered a perfectionist. You must try to see the positive aspects of life, as you must control your mood swings.*

If you were born on the 25th of the month, *you have a need for tranquility and long to be alone. It is important for you to be able to relax and revitalize your mind. You are attracted to the sea, you are very curious, and you are always trying to discover how things work. It is important that you follow your instincts and gain metaphysical knowledge.*

Number of Birthdays 8

If you were born on the 8th, 17th or 26th of the month, your Birthday Number will be 8.

You have a need to be your own boss or, be in a position where you have responsibilities and can supervise others. You are highly motivated by material possessions. You are very confident and ambitious.

***If you were born on the 8th of the month**, you have an incredible magnetic aura around you. Some people find you intimidating. You like to make your own decisions and hate being told what to do.*

Success is very important in your life, and you find happiness in having money and when you strive for material success.

***If you were born on the 17th of the month**, you are ambitious and successful in any business. You have a good memory, but also addictive tendencies. You are sometimes self-centered. You are analytical and need concrete evidence, rather than listening to random information. You are organized and succeed in finance.*

***If you were born on the 26th of the month**, you possess an innate need for balanced relationships. You appreciate your home and family but are almost always too busy to enjoy them. You are happiest when surrounded by animals. You have leadership skills, are organized, but suffer from stress. It is important that you learn to stay calm and manage stressors.*

Number of Birthdays 9

***If you were born on the 9th, 18th or 27th of the
month***, *your Birthday Number is 9.*

*You have a desire to make the world a better place.
You are broad-minded and interested in world
political issues. You can understand people with
different types of thoughts.*

*If you were born on the 9th of the month, your heart is
kind and compassionate. You are idealistic and will
always reach out to those in need. You are reserved
with your personal life, and very creative. You are
sociable and easily attracted. You are a dreamer and
strive to inspire others. Remember to take care of your
health.*

If you were born on the 18th of the month, *you have
the potential to be successful. You are artistic, know
your strengths, are very independent and a leader.
Your tastes are refined, and you need to keep yourself
mentally stimulated. You tend to be disinterested in
worldly things.*

If you were born on the 27th of the month, *you are
very private with your personal life and keep your
emotions to yourself. You are a passionate advocate
for those around you and your communication skills*

are incredible. You have a lot of creativity; you could be a very good writer or composer. You could also be interested in politics.

About the Authors

In addition to her astrological knowledge, Alina A. Rubi has an abundant professional education; she holds certifications in Psychology, Hypnosis, Reiki, Bioenergetic Crystal Healing, Angelic Healing, Dream Interpretation and is a Spiritual Instructor. Rubi has knowledge of Gemology, which she uses to program stones or minerals and turn them into powerful Amulets or Talismans of protection.

Rubi has a practical and purposeful character, which has allowed her to have a special and integrative vision of several worlds, facilitating solutions to specific problems. Alina writes the Monthly Horoscopes for the website of the American Association of Astrologers; you can read them at www.astrologers.com. At this moment she writes a weekly column in the newspaper El Nuevo Herald on spiritual topics, published every Sunday in digital form and on Mondays in print. He also has a program and weekly Horoscope on the YouTube channel of this newspaper. Her Astrological Yearbook is published every year in the newspaper "Diario las Américas", under the column Rubi Astrologa.

Rubi has authored several articles on astrology for the monthly publication "Today's Astrologer", has taught classes on Astrology, Tarot, Palm Reading, Crystal Healing, and Esotericism. She has weekly videos on esoteric topics on her YouTube channel: Rubi Astrologa. She had her own Astrology show broadcasted daily through Flamingo T.V., has been interviewed by several T.V. and radio programs, and every year she publishes her "Astrological Yearbook" with the horoscope sign by sign, and other interesting mystical topics.

She is the author of the books "Rice and Beans for the Soul" Part I, II, and III, a compilation of esoteric articles, published in English, Spanish, French, Italian and Portuguese. "Money for All Pockets", "Love for All Hearts", "Health for All Bodies", Astrological Yearbook 2021, Horoscope 2022, Rituals and Spells for Success in 2022, and 2023 Spells and Secrets, Astrology Classes, Rituals and Charms 2024 and Chinese Horoscope 2024 all available in nine languages: English, Russian, Portuguese, Chinese, Italian, French, Spanish, Japanese and German.

Rubi speaks English and Spanish perfectly, combining all her talents and knowledge in her readings. She currently resides in Miami, Florida.

*For more information you can **visit the website** www.esoterismomagia.com*

Angeline A. Rubi is the daughter of Alina Rubi. She is the editor of all the books. She is currently studying psychology at Florida International University. She is the author of "Protein for Your Mind," a collection of metaphysical articles.

Since she was a child, she has been interested in metaphysical and esoteric subjects, and has practiced astrology and Kabbalah since she was four years old. She has knowledge of Tarot, Reiki, and Gemology.

For more information, please contact her by email: **rubiediciones29@gmail.com**